RELEASE THE STAR WITHIN YOU

GW00728018

www.releasethestarwithinyou.com

RELEASE THE STAR
WITHIN YOU

The essential guide to achieving your dreams and desires
from the performance coach to the stars of media and
entertainment.

WILLIAM PENNINGTON

CHI TEACHING

First published in Great Britain in 2006 by Chi Teaching.

ISBN: 0-9553658-0-5
ISBN: 978-0-9553658-0-5

Publisher: Chi Teaching
http://www.chiteaching.com

Editor: Alison Breach (http://www.sense.me.uk)
Design: Denis Baddeley (http://www.nineninesix.com)
Printing: Lightning Source (http://www.lightningsource.com)

For my stars

Christine for my birthday.

John and Catherine for my life.

Anna, Brian, Dave, Den, Jim, Mike, Steve and Roy for their support during my journey.

Rachel, Katherine and Alice for their inspiration and patience; and for being my wonderful daughters.

Suzanna Bellini, Richard Bandler, John La Valle, John Grinder, Chris Stock, Michael Breen and 'The' Ed Percival for the astonishing learning experiences they created.

My clients who remain anonymous, each a star or a star about to be released.

Alison for her love and encouragement.

Thomas Edison, Inventor:

> *"If we did all the things we are capable of doing, we would literally astound ourselves."*

Contents

Introduction

I've been asking myself what is the difference between the talented people that are successful and those who are not. Some people seem to think the wrong way, use the wrong words and seem unable to take the action they need to. They have star qualities inside, but seem unable to find them when they need them most.

During my journey to becoming a performance coach, I've had many amazing learning experiences. These include a life changing Neuro Linguistic Programming practitioner course in York; training with both the creators of NLP in the same week; studying hypnosis in Los Angeles; and understanding how to be a performance coach from two of the 'masters' in London.

I discovered more while teaching these skills in Spain and London. However the greatest insights of all have come from my clients.

The joy of coaching is working with brilliant people and understanding what they do that makes them so brilliant. In every session I seem to learn something new!

Although I work with people across many industries and job functions, I focus on media and entertainment because it's very competitive with so many people wanting to be stars. I have discovered that performance coaching often delivers results that have an immediate impact.

'Release the star within you' has been inspired by these coaching experiences with successful and future stars of media and entertainment. Where I have referred to clients and quoted the dialogue that occurred between us, these are based on real experiences. However, as coaching is a confidential process, names and stories have been altered to completely protect the anonymity of those clients. Therefore any resemblance to anyone is unintentional and purely coincidental.

How can you use this book to get the most positive results for you?

This guide has been designed to be used as a powerful personal development tool. You could get a notebook, one dedicated to this purpose and write down your answers to the highlighted questions, like the one above.

You will build a picture of your thoughts, goals, values, etc. as you work through the chapters. You could read a chapter each day and build a life changing plan over the next 28 days.

When you first start reading this book, you may think that it appears 'simple' or obvious in places. But remember that most of your behaviours were learned when you were very young and as a result they now take place in your unconscious mind. As you start to question these 'simple' but fundamental habits, you will begin to make a significant difference to your life.

The physicist Albert Einstein defined insanity as:

"doing the same thing over and over again and expecting different results."

Yet sometimes we still expect things to change without us having to do anything new or different. When you answer the questions, do the visualisations and exercises in this book, you will create new possibilities to change.

William Pennington
wp@releasethestarwithinyou.com

CHAPTER 1

Taking the first step

One of my favourite quotes is by the philosopher, Peter Ouspensky:

> *"The chief obstacle to the attainment of self-awareness is we think we have it."*

Philosophers and psychologists have always talked about the importance of self-awareness. You might well be asking "Why do I need self-awareness?"

The latest scientific thinking about intelligence is that EQ (the measure of Emotional Intelligence) is more important to success than the more famous IQ (the measure of cognitive intelligence). We all know people who have a very high IQ, but don't seem to cope with life's journey.

Scientists measured a large sample of people to understand the average level of EQ, what they found was that the more experience and older people were, the higher their EQ was.

This is very different from IQ which is pretty much fixed for your adult life. This is also great news because it proves that we can actively develop our Emotional Intelligence!

If EQ is the key to achievement, then emotional self-awareness is the foundation to that success.

The stories and questions in this book are about gaining self-awareness. Questions like these help you build a clearer picture of you:

Where are you going?

What is important about that to you?

What will that say about you when you get there?

How can you use this self-awareness to help you achieve your dreams and desires? Perhaps for you it's recognising you already have the skills and resources you need to achieve what you want; or maybe you are holding on to some limiting belief that prevents you from moving forward; or you may find what is currently lacking for you to be motivated to take action.

Whichever it is, the questions in this book will create additional self-awareness for you. This is just the start of your journey.

So throughout your life, you can increase your self-awareness, your overall Emotional Intelligence and with that, your capability for success.

CHAPTER 2

Write down your goals!

It has been well known for some time that having goals is a very important aspect of human life. The ancient Greek philosopher Aristotle said:

"Man is a goal-seeking animal. His life only has meaning if he is reaching out and striving for his goals."

The advice to 'write down your goals' may seem like the simplest you could be given. I think you'll be amazed to hear, that when asked this question how few respond they have recently done it and how many have actually never done it. Whilst investigating student development, researchers found that only 3 students out of the 600 being studied were certain of their goals and had actually written them down.

I am even more amazed when I see the effect of doing just that. My client Andrea, who is a talented actress wanted to get her first starring role in a feature film. After writing down specifically what she wanted, within a few months she had been presented with three suitable opportunities and an offer of the significant part in a US production!

When did you last write down your personal goals? Successful businesses are constantly reviewing and refining their targets, yet research has shown that less than 5% of us take this approach to our own lives.

Maybe now it's time to think:

What is there in your life that you still want to have 10 years from now?

Imagine all the new things that you could do and the dreams and desires you can achieve in that time.

And write them down, now!

And what of those students? When studied thirty years later, the 3 were more financially successful than the other 597 put together!

Benjamin Mays, an educator who gave the eulogy for Rev. Martin Luther King said:

> "The tragedy of life doesn't lie in not reaching your goal. The tragedy lies in having no goal to reach."

CHAPTER 3

Creating the full picture

Once you start to write down your dreams and desires, you may begin to think about these goals in more detail, because as you create more detail, you make the dream more real and therefore more achievable.

What specifically do you want to achieve?

How specifically will you have achieved that?

I ask these questions to get as much detail as I can from my clients.

I was coaching Ben, a theatrical director and we were talking about his 10 year goals:

Client: I want to direct a show at the 'National'.

Coach: What show specifically do you want to direct?

Client: I want to direct a show that is my own production at the 'National' that will be created in a collaborative, multi-skilled way; with well known actors; the best designers; lighting and movement. The show will be nominated for an Olivier Award for best show or director; will sell out and get a fantastic reaction from the audience. The production will be an ensemble piece, created by a team effort, comedic in nature, including lots of 'stuff that works' for the performers and the audience.

Coach: What 'stuff that works' specifically?

Client: Stuff well done; a story well told; clarity; places not been; originality.

Coach: How specifically will it have originality?

Client: Leadership, energy, direction, comedy – make it funny.

You may have noticed that as you drill into more detail you get fewer words. That's good because you are now getting to the core of your goals. When it becomes harder to get more detail, then you probably have enough.

Keynote speaker and productivity consultant, Dr. Denis Waitley says:

> "The reason most people never reach their goals is that they don't define them, or ever seriously consider them as believable or achievable. Winners can tell you where they are going, what they plan to do along the way, and who will be sharing the adventure with them."

CHAPTER 4

Considering new perspectives

While you are creating lots of detail around your goals, it's sometimes useful to consider another perspective.

In Craig's case who is an actor, defining the exact type of production he wanted to be in was proving difficult. While coaching, I asked specific questions to enable him to get another perspective on his goals.

Who do you aspire to be like?

Whose work do you admire?

Which fellow professionals would you like to work with?

He answered these and thereby developed a list of directors and producers whose work he liked and with whom he would like to work.

You may find you would like to be the next Cary Grant, after all, as Cary Grant once said:

"Everyone wants to be Cary Grant. Even I want to be Cary Grant!"

While you are considering the achievements of others, ask yourself how they made their success happen and build a more detailed picture of your own goals as a result.

Once Craig had created very specific goals, both in terms of the type of work he wanted and the people he wanted to work with, it became much easier to write his biography, build his website, create his showreel, brief his agent and target the right producers and directors.

Within a few months he was getting the exact type of work he wanted with the award winning producers and directors that he so admired.

Leonardo da Vinci; architect, anatomist, sculptor, engineer, inventor, geometer, musician and painter said:

"All our knowledge has its origins in our perceptions."

He was also a life-long vegetarian and believed it was wrong to kill animals in order to eat them. It is interesting to note his perception was such that his painting of 'The Last Supper' only shows bread and fruits on the table!

CHAPTER 5

Committing to a date

Committing to a completion date may appear to be obvious advice and it seems simple, but in practice it can be the hardest thing to do.

It's very easy to be unspecific about finishing something. We find lots of words to avoid being specific: 'soon, later, eventually, next few years/months/weeks/days, in a while, in due course, in time, etc.'

How often do people say "Yes, I will do that by noon on the 10th January 2012"?

A former client, Daniel, who is a musician and song writer, was writing a musical which he had been working on for five years. Not surprisingly, he really wanted to finish it! Our conversation went like this:

Coach: When will you finish this?

Client: Soon.

Coach: When do you want to finish this by?

Client: This year sometime.

Coach: What day specifically will you have finished this by?

Client: Christmas Eve.

Coach: This year?

Client: Yes! My project will be finished by Christmas Eve this year!

If you think of a goal that seems not to get completed, make a commitment with yourself to achieve that by a specific

date. Imagine that you are sometime after that; a few days or even a few years. Now look back at your completed goal.

How good does it feel now to have accomplished your goal?

Daniel returned from his mental journey to Christmas Day with a big smile on his face. He was now motivated to complete his musical by Christmas Eve as he had committed.

And yes, he did complete it!

RELEASE THE STAR WITHIN YOU

Chapter 6

Knowing when to celebrate

You have made plans for your future and you have set out your dreams and desires; then you have added more detail and target dates. Now before you begin your journey:

How will you know when you have reached your goals?

This can be a particularly tricky question to answer in the media and entertainment world, where simply having your screenplay made into a film; or having a leading role in a play; or your article being published may not be sufficient on its own. Often I hear words like successful, good, great, fabulous, loved, acclaimed, etc. When I do, I always want my client to have more specific information.

I was coaching a journalist, Ellen, who was also writing a novel and her goal was for this to be published within two years:

Client: I will be happy when the work sells and gets critical acclaim.

Coach: What sort of acclaim?

Client: I want people to like the work.

Coach: Who specifically will 'like the work'?

Client: There are literary critics who could review the book; a couple in particular that are prestigious and good reviews by them would be wonderful.

Coach: Anyone else?

Client: But what would be really great is to have the people who buy the book really love it.

I was thinking about Ellen's desire to have her booked loved and wanted to see how she would know this to be true:

Coach: How will you know that they *really love it*?

Client: When I have received some emails from satisfied readers or met them at a book signing.

Coach: What would they say?

As a big smile crept across Ellen's face, I knew that she knew enough to know when she had reached her goal.

Think of a goal that is particularly important to you, and imagine for a moment that you have achieved it.

What has happened for you to consider that an achievement?

Who else has acknowledged it and how did they do that?

How did you know when it reached the standards you set for yourself?

Knowing how you will know when you have achieved not only creates more detail now, but it also gives you a fuller sense of achievement later. That way you will also know when to celebrate!

Tom Peters, author of the 'greatest business book of all time' says:

"Celebrate what you want to see more of."

CHAPTER 7

Being focused

Sometimes there can be a little too much creativity in the media and entertainment industry and I often see this when clients have taken on too many projects, without having the resources to finish them. This is often exasperated by the fact that they are self-employed and don't want to say 'no' to anyone.

My approach to this situation is to review each project in the light of long term goals and values. This gives a new perspective and allows them to decide on priorities, so that they can decline or delay some options.

The historian, Arnold J Toynbee said:

> "It is a paradoxical but profoundly true and important principle of life that the most likely way to reach a goal is to be aiming not at that goal itself but at some more ambitious goal beyond it."

I was working with Ben, one of my most creative clients, who applied this concept to all his projects. Each time he took on a new job, he would automatically extrapolate it forward to a new long term ambitious goal. The result was that he was going to be the best writer, director and producer in radio, TV, theatre and film!

What specific job and sector do you want to be a star in?

Of course, there are people who have become successful in multiple areas, the most dazzling like Leonardo da Vinci are called 'polymaths', but most became accomplished in one role before diversifying.

It's very tempting to keep all your options open and sometimes this may be necessary. Although how can you make decisions on priorities if you have no clear vision on the overall direction you want to take? Or in Ben's case, who was seriously over committed, which jobs to take and which to leave.

Of course as new opportunities present themselves, you can decide to refine your longer term goals. However if you find this is happening all the time, you could ask yourself how committed you are to your longer term vision?

As Lewis Carroll wrote:

> *"One day Alice came to a fork in the road and saw a Cheshire cat in a tree. "Which road do I take?" she asked. "Where do you want to go?" was his response. "I don't know" Alice answered. "Then," said the cat, "it doesn't matter."*

Ben decided that what he really loved was theatre and his goal was to become a leading theatrical director.

Within a few months and with this precise focus he gained from the decision, he was employed to direct one of the largest theatrical productions in the UK.

CHAPTER 8

Discover your passions

Discovering the things that you are passionate about can have some dramatic effects.

Felix (a writer) had many different projects on the go including a novel, three film scripts and two factual books! We had spent some time discussing his priorities and in particular the novel.

Over the weeks we discussed his short, medium and long term goals. We talked about his working habits and what patterns resulted in a good writing flow.

Sometimes you can miss the things that are really important about yourself. One of the benefits of having a coach is that they notice everything. I had noticed that every now and again Felix mentioned poetry, but always last and as an aside to his other activities.

So in one session I asked him questions about his poetry and as he explained I witnessed a transformation in his body language and mood. As we explored this aspect of his creative life, he came to the realisation that poetry represented the core of everything he does, from his desire to create poetic films, to his passion to create 'passion' in others.

Felix said "All art aspires to the condition of music, and poetry is one step away." Within days he had begun to write poetry again and within a few weeks had completed two of his other writing projects.

What are the activities that you are passionate about?

How important are they to you?

How much energy could you gain from doing them?

What happens when you don't do them for a long time?

I have observed and experienced that some activities give you energy and some take it away. Discover what activities give you positive energy and make sure you spend more time on them. For me it's playing my saxophone.

One of the world's greatest ever saxophonists, Charlie Parker said:

> *"Music is your own experience, your own thoughts, your wisdom. If you don't live it, it won't come out of your horn. They teach you there's a boundary line to music. But, man, there's no boundary line to art."*

CHAPTER 9

Creating a clear vision

You may read some 'self help' books that talk about vision, but what exactly is a vision? Sometimes they ask about your 'life purpose' and maybe for you that is clear, but for many that's something they are still searching for.

So how do you create a vision big enough to excite and motivate you, but one that's realistic enough for you to believe you can achieve it?

I work with all of my clients to create a clear vision of their future, that they will love. Ben wants to become a leading theatrical director; Nicola desires to move her career from TV to Film; Gwyneth wants to make regular commercially successful and critically acclaimed feature films; Ellen would love to receive great reviews for her latest novel; and Isabel dreams of winning a major award.

I like the way the film maker, George Lucas put it:

"You have to find something that you love enough to be able to take risks, jump over the hurdles and break through the brick walls that are always going to be placed in front of you. If you don't have that kind of feeling for what it is you're doing, you'll stop at the first giant hurdle."

What would your goals look like if they were 'one step beyond' where they are now?

When you have gone those extra steps – where will you be?

I was coaching Andrea, an actress and looking to clarify her vision:

Coach: What if it were possible to have anything you could wish for?

Client: Anything? (with a big smile)

Coach: Yes, anything you desire.

Client: The Oscar for Best Actress.

She described the event when she won the award and how she would feel about that happening:

Coach: And what is beyond that?

Client: Mmm. Interesting! I have a story that I want to tell!

We discussed her adoption story and her desire to share that experience. She realised that her long term future would be on both sides of the camera. We are waiting for her award, but Andrea is already pursuing this new dimension to her film making career.

Your clear vision can stretch you so you can aim higher and achieve your dreams. John F. Kennedy, former President of the USA said:

> *"The problems of the world cannot possibly be solved by sceptics or cynics whose horizons are limited by the obvious realities. We need men and women who can dream of things that never were."*

CHAPTER 10

Getting unstuck

Sometimes we all feel stuck on the immediate decisions, issues and plans; and lose sight of the longer term. The benefit of working with a performance coach is that they always remember the power of the perspective of time.

My client Gwyneth is a producer and we were discussing the immediate issues that she needed to overcome; primarily the big change of career from a salaried job to setting up her own TV production company. We were talking in some depth about the decision that was looming and the next 12 months:

Coach: How will you know when it's the right time to make the decision?

Client: I'm *just* not sure when to make the move.

You may notice that she used the word *'just'*, which tells us that she may be stuck and only seeing a single solution.

Coach: Where will this lead in five and ten years?

Client: In five years time the company will have been very successful and I'll be looking to sell it and by ten years I'll have moved on to a new project.

Coach: How does the current situation look from the perspective of where you will be in ten years time?

Client: Differently. (she mused)

In that one moment the decision seemed obvious – Gwyneth knew that she could wait for the opportune moment to leave her current job and meanwhile she would continue to prepare for the following years of business.

You may now be thinking about your current issues and decisions that you feel stuck on. But just for a moment, stop and consider your long term goals.

Imagine you have achieved these goals, how will it feel to be celebrating your achievements?

Imagine looking back through your journey, what are the steps that have brought you to this place?

How do your current short term issues and decisions look?

Now when you put things in perspective, decisions on the next steps and the short term objectives and priorities become much clearer.

The nineteenth century orator, Robert Green Ingersoll said:

> *"In the presence of eternity, the mountains are as transient as the clouds."*

CHAPTER 11

Motivating yourself

The author Louis Boone said:

> *"Don't fear failure so much that you refuse to try new things. The saddest summary of a life contains three descriptions: could have, might have and should have."*

Of all the precise words that we use, the most revealing about how we are motivated are those called 'modal operators'. Some of these words suggest we possibly will take action (I *might*, I *could*, I *may*, I *can*); some suggest we feel it is necessary to take action (I *should*, I *must*, I *ought*); and others suggest it is desirable to take action (I *love* to, I *want* to, I *like* to).

Now think of something that you may be putting off doing; what words are you trying to use to motivate yourself?

I was coaching Henry, who is a film director, regarding changing his agent, as he didn't feel that his current one was right for him; despite being one of the biggest and best known. Our conversation went something like this:

Client: I really *should* change!

Coach: What's stopping you?

Client: I've weighed up the pros and cons of changing agent a number of times and I really *want* to change.

Coach: This doesn't seem enough for you to take some action. So what will happen if you don't do this?

Client: The consequences are too painful to consider. I really *need* to change.

…and he did.

Of course, each individual is different. The words that motivated Henry may not be the ones that will motivate you. Think about the tasks that you are putting off and use different words; you will discover that you feel differently about each of them. Simply by changing *"I should"* to *"I must"* or *"I want"* may be what it takes to motivate you to take action.

Dr. Denis Waitley, keynote speaker and productivity consultant, said:

"The winners in life think constantly in terms of I can, I will and I am. Losers, on the other hand, concentrate their waking thoughts on what they should have or would have done, or what they can't do."

You may be thinking now about the words you use; change them and you change your mind; change your mind and you change your actions; change your actions and you change your life.

Being self-motivated

We believe that successful people have high self-motivation. But what is it? And what happens when you say "*I have no motivation!*"?

The interesting thing about this statement is the actual words that are being used:

Client: I have no motivation.

Coach: It's your lucky day, I have a new stock of motivation just arrived from the States and you can have as much of it as you like!

The problem is that we pretend 'motivation' exists even though in reality it doesn't; and of course, it is impossible to find more of something that doesn't exist!

What has happened is that we have taken the action of '*being motivated*' and turned it into an object '*motivation*'. This is called a 'nominalisation'.

The effect of using the word *'motivation'* is to prevent us from moving forward. It will help if you simply start thinking and talking about *'being motivated'*.

Psychologists say that you either move towards a goal you want or away from something you don't want.

So if you're not being self-motivated,

What is stopping you taking action?

What are the consequences of not taking action?

Earlier we talked about motivating words like 'I *love* to, I *want* to, I *like* to'. I like to use the word *desire*.

How do you feel when you desire something? Is that enough to motivate you to take action?

How do you feel when you hate something? How more or less are you motivated now?

And as Tony Robbins, motivational speaker and author, says:

"In life you need either inspiration or desperation."

Which will motivate you? Will you be inspired to achieve your dreams and desires or desperate to avoid the opposite? Either way you can now be motivated to take the action you need to become one of those highly self-motivated successful people.

CHAPTER 13

Become more motivated

Do you take words for granted? I believe most of us do and what I mean by this is that we assume everyone attaches the same meaning to words as we do. Most of the time this assumption makes our communication easier and quicker, but sometimes it results in miscommunication and misunderstanding.

As a coach, I listen to every word my clients say, because sometimes just one word has a very special meaning and can unlock a client's potential.

I was working with Ellen, a journalist and novelist who was struggling to be motivated to write. We were exploring what it will mean to her to finish and publish her novel. I was interested in the reason this project meant so much to her.

There's a question (or a variant of it) that I tend to ask quite a lot in my coaching, which is "What will that mean for you?"

The answer I get back is important but the individual words are crucial because they are attached to the client's values. I then drill deeper and deeper into the responses and deeper into their values. I keep going until the phrases get simpler, often honing them down to one word.

Sometimes the word gets a bit too 'woolly', for example:

Client: Happiness.

Coach: When you have happiness, what will that mean for you?

Client: I'll be happy!

With Ellen it wasn't working! I was looking for a word, that represented a value, that would 'light' her up. I tried another tack:

Coach: What are the novels that inspire you?

Client: …

Coach: What do you love about them?

Client: …

Coach: What do they mean for you?

Client: …

In her responses, one word struck me as being important. So I asked what it would be like if her novel meant 'that' to her readers. As she thought about my question, a huge smile crossed her face and I knew we had found a key value for her.

The word was 'solace' and this reminds me of what the psychiatrist, Carl Jung said about creativity:

> "The creation of something new is not accomplished by the intellect but by the play instinct acting from inner necessity. The creative mind plays with the objects it loves."

After this session Ellen's novel returned to being an object of love that she soon completed.

CHAPTER 14

Having positive thoughts

When you think about yourself; are you optimistic or pessimistic? Winston Churchill, former British Prime Minister and author said:

> "The optimist sees opportunity in every danger and the pessimist sees danger in every opportunity."

Do you see the glass as half empty or half full? Or perhaps it's twice as large as it needs to be!

Psychologists realised that they tended to spend most of their efforts focused on problems and issues, so now a new field called positive psychology is emerging. They are making some interesting discoveries. For instance when they studied a group of nuns, they found that the optimists outlived the pessimists by over 10 years!

In another survey they asked a group of students to count the number of pictures in a newspaper. On the second page there was an advert that said "Don't read any further there are 42 pictures!" What's interesting is that none of the pessimists noticed or paid attention to the advert, while all the optimists took the advice.

I have noticed that we all have a mix of optimistic and pessimistic tendencies. I was working with Isabel, a writer/director and during each session I noticed something particular about her; she almost always said 'If' before every future goal:

Client: If I finish my script... If I find a producer... If I get funding...

So we explored what was happening and it transpired that she always considered ALL the possible outcomes fully, weighing up ALL the pros and cons, making sure she was fully ready for both success and failure.

I was curious and asked how it was possible for both positive and negative outcomes to occur? Isabel thought for a while and then had a 'light bulb moment'. She realised that almost half of her energy was being spent on outcomes that didn't happen.

I asked her which of the outcomes she would like to occur and of course, she wanted the positive ones. By the next session instead of constantly saying the word 'If' she was now using the word 'When':

Client: When I finish my script. When I find a producer. When I get funding.

Consequently Isabel moved forward with her plans to make her film.

How much time do you spend thinking about things that will go right for you?

How much time do you spend thinking or maybe even worrying about what may go wrong?

How do you feel now about the balance and what will happen when you spend more of your time thinking positively?

Dr David Schwartz, author of 'The Magic of Thinking Big' said:

"Believe it can be done. When you believe something can be done, really believe, your mind will find the ways to do it. Believing a solution paves the way to solution."

CHAPTER 15

Dealing with failure

The founder of the Ford Motor Company, Henry Ford said:

"Failure is only the opportunity to begin again more intelligently."

In the media and entertainment industry, as in many others, there is intense competition. As a result you may find that you are not selected for every project or that not all your projects come to fruition. However as one opportunity closes so another one opens, each bringing you closer to the goals that you have set yourself (and have written down).

Isabel (the writer/director) was visiting a funding organisation to meet with her former boss, who was now a senior director there. She was looking for funding for an animated feature film and felt this was going to be a very useful meeting. She had set some high expectations for it, but came away very disappointed with the outcome, because the director had seemed to ignore her for most of the meeting. He had even taken a phone call and left the room at one point. This surprised me, but made me wonder if I had the whole picture:

Coach: Who else was in the meeting?

Client: My former boss had bought along their Head of Animation.

Coach: How was that person relevant to you?

Client: That's why I was there! I want to get my film funded.

Coach: What does this introduction say about what your former boss thinks of you?

She paused and thought:

Client: I guess it shows he respects my work, he feels comfortable to introduce me to a colleague and he was trying to help in the best way he thought possible.

Isabel realised that she now had a new and useful connection to help her bring her project closer to fruition.

Consider all the possible outcomes from a meeting or other activity. Even if an outcome may seem negative at first, there is always an opportunity to learn and have some feedback that takes you forward towards your goals.

How would your approach be different now that you think about any outcome in a more positive light?

Richard Bandler, who is the co-developer of Neuro Linguistic Programming (NLP) says:

"The great thing about the past is that it is over and the best thing about the future is that it is full of limitless possibilities."

Always be open to all those possibilities.

CHAPTER 16

Overcoming your fears

I was coaching John, an executive with an advertising company, who had to stand up and make a presentation about his organisation to an audience of 1000+ people. This prospect might fill even an experienced presenter with some anxious thoughts. But he was terrified!

We have fears of all sorts of things that in fact we have no reason to fear. It is very unlikely that a spider or mouse will represent any danger to you, but phobias such as these, can cripple us in certain situations.

While undertaking my NLP training, I learned how to cure a phobia in less than one hour. So when I came home I was very keen to try out my new skills. My daughter had been terrified of dogs since she was a child. She can't remember the incident, but has a scar just below her left eye that she got when she was eighteen months old.

After just a few minutes of a specific visualisation technique, her phobia was cured and she can now enjoy being with a friendly dog.

With John, I used another sort of visualisation. In a nutshell, I asked him to create a video of his performance, experienced from the audience's point of view and use the feedback he gained from that perspective to improve his performance.

This visualisation will work best when you are sitting in a comfortable place, so you can be relaxed. Think of something that you really want it to go well.

What would that look and sound like if it is happening right now and what would a video of that be like in your mind?

Now step outside yourself and observe it happening from the outside, what changes would you make to improve your performance or the result?

Keep refining it until you feel happy with your performance. When you are completely happy, re-run the video over and over again.

How many times have you run through it?

Are you sure?

Count them again!

Once John had run through his performance many times, his anxiety had substantially reduced and he was ready to give a brilliant account of his company.

Roger Staubach, American Football legend observed:

"Spectacular achievements are always preceded by painstaking preparation."

CHAPTER 17

Preparing properly

When you have an important meeting, some say the most important aspects are the planning and preparation. But how often do we really do that?

There is a powerful technique that I use with clients who need to get ready for that important meeting or encounter. For Olivia, an actress, that meeting was with her agent.

For this technique it makes the exercise easier if you position two chairs facing each other. Then stand looking at the two chairs and imagine the setting in which the meeting will take place. See yourself in one chair and the other person in the other.

When you have a detailed picture of the scene, go over and sit in your chair. Take a while to think about your perspective.

What outcomes do you want from the meeting?

What information do you want the other person to gain?

How do you want to have influenced them?

Next imagine the meeting taking place and run through the conversation in your mind.

When you have finished, stand up, shake off (literally shake your body) and sit in the other chair, as the other person. Imagine you are the other person and have their perspective. What do you now want from the meeting? However odd it may seem, answer these questions with 'I'.

Now imagine the meeting taking place again, this time from the other person's perspective. Run through the conversation again. Once you have finished stand up and shake off again.

The next stage is to stand and look at the two chairs and take on the role of an independent observer, coach or maybe film director. Hear and see the conversation taking place between these two people, from a completely detached perspective. Ask yourself how you would improve that meeting and what advice you would give yourself about this encounter.

Now finally sit back in the first chair and be yourself again. You have now had the experience of seeing it from the other person's perspective and you have received some independent advice.   Ask yourself how you will now approach this meeting differently.

Olivia took her 'own' advice, had a successful meeting with her agent and started to get the auditions she wanted.

The author, William A. Ward said there are:

"4 steps to achievement: plan purposefully, prepare prayerfully, proceed positively, pursue persistently"

CHAPTER 18

Removing limitations

None of us truly know the limit of our capabilities. Some don't believe they are amazing and are capable of much more. You hear people say "I can't do that" or "I'll never be able to do that" all the time.

Most people believe they are not able to do certain things. Of course there may be some physical limits to what your body can accomplish, but most of the time we have mental limits that are far lower.

Remember there was a time when you learned to walk and you learned to talk. Just imagine what else you could learn now.

How much more room do you have for learning?

Next time you catch yourself limiting yourself, just add one little word …YET. For example, 'I can't do this YET' tells you (and others) that you will be able to do this one day.

As the poet T.S. Eliot said:

> *"Only those who risk going too far can possibly find out how far one can go."*

You may believe that some things are just impossible. But how do we know what the possible limits are?

In 1954 the world believed that it was impossible for a human being to run a mile in less than four minutes and for years many had tried, come close, but failed.

One man, Roger Bannister, believed differently and broke not only the record but the very limiting belief of the world. It may surprise you to hear that within months, dozens of runners could now beat his new world record.

Roger Bannister wrote the following about his experience:

> *"No longer conscious of my movement, I discovered a new unity with nature. I had found a new source of power and beauty, a source I never dreamt existed."*

Some may even believe that they are not worthy of achieving their dreams and desires. Although they may not realise this.

Ask yourself "Do you deserve to achieve your goals?" and if you don't believe you do, then ask yourself:

What would you need to change for you to deserve to achieve your goals?

Who does believe that you deserve to achieve your goals?

I believe that you have enormous potential inside you. That's why I have an affinity for the Thomas Edison quote on 'My stars' page. It's also hanging on my office wall and is worthy of being repeated again and again:

"If we all did the things we are capable of doing, we would literally astound ourselves."

Go ahead and astound yourself!

CHAPTER 19

Discovering star-qualities

I believe that everyone is brilliant; all of us have the capability to achieve amazing things, way beyond our expectations. As the young author Anne Frank so eloquently put it:

> *"Everyone has inside themselves a piece of good news! The good news is that you really don't know how great you can be, how much you can love, what you can accomplish, and what your potential is!"*

As I work with my clients I am looking to discover their star qualities, their pieces of brilliance and amplify them. Sometimes this happens very explicitly. I had agreed with Ben (the theatrical director) to spend a session removing his 'bushel'.

As I write this I am asking myself where does the saying 'hiding your light under a bushel' come from and what is a bushel anyway? I discovered the saying comes from the New Testament (Matthew 5:15):

"Neither do men light a candle, and put it under a bushel, but on a candlestick."

Apparently a bushel in this context is a basket capable of holding 64 dry pints!

However for Ben, it must have been a pretty huge basket! We spent the whole session exploring his achievements, what he has done well, and what he was most pleased with.

Think back through your life and remember the times when you did things that you loved doing. Now think of the things you've done that worked out well.

What are the things that you have achieved?

Remember all your successes, however small they may seem to you. Get a large piece of paper and write them down. Better still, tell someone else and get them to write them down for you.

Now I know that in some countries (including my own) this sort of behaviour is sometimes frowned upon. We have a saying 'blowing you own trumpet' to try to demean those that celebrate their achievements.

Well when we celebrated Ben's achievements the effect was transformational. At one point he recalled a time when he was only seventeen and was asked to direct a production with a group of special needs teenagers. He told me how he used his unique approach to collaborative theatre production to get this group to create their own piece. "They loved working this way and were inspired by my approach", he said "the resulting play was an inspiration to them and their families."

For weeks afterwards Ben was remembering all the small and big achievements from his life – and these became the foundation for us to build his amazing future as a leading theatrical director.

Now that you can sit and look at your own achievements written out, what else is possible in your future?

Oprah Winfrey, TV presenter, publisher and philanthropist says:

> *"The more you praise and celebrate your life, the more there is in life to celebrate."*

CHAPTER 20

Challenging your beliefs

The belief that 'beliefs are changeable' is in itself a challenging belief to many!

Our beliefs are critical in determining our behaviour, our performance and our contentment with life. We often think in terms of 'having a belief' or 'holding on to one', as if they are real.

What beliefs did you have as a child that you now know not to be true?

And which of your beliefs do you have now that you believe you will still have when you are older?

Now you may be wondering if beliefs are in fact moveable or perhaps even changeable. Do we leave them behind or outgrow them?

I find it most useful to think of beliefs as either being limiting or empowering.

Here are just a few of the limiting beliefs I have encountered in the media and entertainment industry:

Client: I can't contact producers and directors directly.

Client: I cannot be successful in the industry unless I make it in Hollywood.

Client: The only way we can raise money is to have our business plan approved by lawyers and accountants.

Client: The other people applying for this position will all have much more experience than me.

The author Norman Vincent Peale said:

> *"People become really quite remarkable when they start thinking that they can do things. When they believe in themselves they have the first secret of success."*

I ask my clients to think about how useful these limiting beliefs are and how they help them achieve their goals. Then I ask them to create more empowering beliefs:

Client: I need to network amongst the widest possible circle to further my career.

Client: Hollywood is just one of many avenues for me to pursue my goals.

Client: We can raise funding by looking at all the options and checking with multiple sources.

Client: My experience is very relevant for this job and other applicants will have completely different experience.

What are your limiting beliefs?

How would you change them to empowering ones?

One of the empowering beliefs of high performance coaching is that 'There is no failure, only feedback'. If you think of the times when things haven't gone as well as you expected or even when you considered you had failed.

How much did you learn from those experiences?

I believe that everything can be considered an achievement if you have learned from it.

What do you now believe?

CHAPTER 21

Don't give up

You may be thinking that the advice to not give up is obvious but wondering how could you put this into practice.

I quoted George Lucas in an earlier chapter, but it's worth repeating here what he said:

> *"You have to find something that you love enough to be able to take risks, jump over the hurdles and break through the brick walls that are always going to be placed in front of you. If you don't have that kind of feeling for what it is you're doing, you'll stop at the first giant hurdle."*

My client Kate was running a production of a play and things were not going smoothly. There had been problems with the venue, problems finding actors and just when things seemed to be coming together, with less than a week to go, she lost both her leading actors. She almost gave in there and then, but the idea of not doing this production after all her efforts was too much to bear. She told me "I will just carry on until I know it's either too late or I turn into a screaming lunatic!"

In writing this book I had major writer's block, which is a little ironic as I have coached many writers through similar issues. I found coaching myself through this barrier very difficult! Which reminded me of the saying 'cobblers have the worst shoes in the village'!

When you come across your barriers ask yourself the following questions:

What do you really want and what will it mean for you when you have it?

Imagine yourself having this now, how did you get there and how good does it feel to have reached your goals?

I used this approach and imagined myself in my new home and working in the way I wanted. I made the image as vivid as I could.

I awoke this morning thinking of Thomas Edison's quote:

> *"Many of life's failures are people who did not realise how close they were to success when they gave up."*

! am writing this chapter at 4am and I feel I am over my giant hurdle!

Kate's production got re-scheduled to one week later, July 7th 2005. A date that many of us will not forget! But she was not going to be outdone by terrorists and re-scheduled her performance again for two weeks later.

During that day another incident unfolded, but the production still went ahead. Kate said *"It was a wonderful night and I was overwhelmed by it all. I still feel happy about it."* The success of the evening had motivated her to reach her next hurdle.

CHAPTER 22

Selling yourself

Imagine you are in a hotel lift on the top floor and in walks Stephen Spielberg (or whoever else could be the most useful person to meet in your career). You say hello and he asks what you do. Often people do one of two things; they freeze and say nothing (or nonsense) or they tell him their life story. Neither is a helpful approach!

This is how the Americans came up with the saying an 'elevator pitch', I guess the British version 'lift pitch' doesn't quite sound the same. The premise is that a business idea should be communicable in the time it takes to travel a few floors.

Creating one can be quite challenging! In the film industry they create 'high concept' pitches to convey a new project. For example, 'Batman meets The Waltons' – now that would be an odd TV series!

If you were to describe yourself by mixing two characters from your peers and predecessors, who would you choose?

My role as a coach involves asking many questions to find the root cause of my client's issues, so would I be 'David Letterman meets Michael Parkinson'? My client, Andrea described herself as 'Meryl Streep meets Maggie Smith'.

The 'high concept' pitch is useful for your own self-awareness and branding but your elevator pitch is more useful as it is what you might say at a party, a networking event, or in a lift.

Write down what you do on a page (or more) and then edit it down to a paragraph. Learn it and practice it. You never know when it might be useful!

Now try that 'high concept' pitch again, who are you now?

As I am writing this personal development book to bring the power of coaching to many, maybe I will be described as 'Tom Peters meets Paul McKenna'!?

When you think about your 'high concept' pitch again, what does that say about who you want to become?

Understanding your values

A 'high concept' pitch is useful for self-awareness and an 'elevator pitch' is useful for making others aware of who we are, what we do and where we are going. When you understand your values you begin to explain why you are doing things.

I was working with Liam, a TV writer/director and we were talking around his business and what it meant to him. As we explored the values behind his goals, I kept asking the questions "What will that mean for you?" and "When you have achieved that, what sort of person will that make you?"

He started to look at his core values "my work is about humour but more than that…" and in just a few minutes he came up with the perfect description of his work "comedy with a kick" (*changed for confidentiality reasons*).

You too can explore your values with a simple but powerful two-step process.

Step one is to ask yourself when you have achieved your goals, what will that mean for you. Write down the values that you think of.

Step two is to look at the values you have written down and think when you have achieved those values what will that mean for you?

Just keep repeating step two until you have run out of steam or you begin to repeat yourself! Now look at your values.

Think about how you could use these values to build a 'mission statement' or use a phrase or words to make a strap-line for your business.

One of my values that resonated with me was "heart felt". As a result I used it to create the new strap-line for my coaching company: 'Chi Coaching: at the heart of performance'.

As Liam thought about his new phrase – he had a large smile on his face and declared that it would become the new strap-line for his company and a way of explaining the difference in his work.

The author Henry David Thoreau said:

> "Live your beliefs and you can turn the world around."

CHAPTER 24

Listening carefully

In the 'Guide to Good Leadership', Kenneth A. Wells said:

"A good listener tries to understand thoroughly what the other person is saying. In the end he may disagree sharply, but before he disagrees, he wants to know exactly what it is he is disagreeing with."

You may have heard the saying 'you have one mouth and two ears and should use them in that proportion!' However I believe we have one mouth, two ears and billions of brain cells and must use them in that proportion!

Recently I was reminded of the significance of this when teaching a group of new coaches about questioning. I had set an exercise to teach listening skills; after all until you have listened to a client, how can you know what questions to ask. The task was to listen to one sentence from the 'client', then repeat the sentence back word-for-word and have them write down exactly what they had heard.

I was listening in on one couple: the client said "I would like to have…", then the trainee coach repeated back "I wouldn't like to have…" The complete opposite meaning. But then the client also completely misheard and wrote down "I would like to have…" and said to the trainee coach "That was right"!

Some people recommend that you paraphrase what you hear (i.e. use your own words to summarise what was said) and say it back to the speaker to prove you have heard and understood them.

This can be a powerful way to communicate but the flaw with this approach is that the exact words people say are important because we all think and use words in different ways.

In high performance coaching, listening is one of the most important skills, utilising all those billions of brain cells to hear and understand every word; because every word counts. I usually prefer to 'parrot-phrase', reflecting back the exact words a client uses. Often the result is that the client looks puzzled and thinks "Mmmm. Did I really say that?"

How much do you listen?

How much of the time are you just waiting to speak?

What difference will it make to your communications when the other person knows you are truly listening?

The author Ernest Hemingway said

> *"I like to listen. I have learned a great deal from listening carefully. Most people never listen."*

Learn to listen carefully and you too will be amazed by what you learn!

CHAPTER 25

Networking effectively

"If one more person tells me to network, I will simply scream" said Craig (the actor). He seemed to be reflecting a theme that I often hear from my clients about networking.

Just in case you have missed this phenomenon, 'networking' is a way of creating and expanding your contacts for your professional advantage. You can achieve this through clubs, events, social gatherings, etc. Some of these can be specific industry events; some are even created specifically for networking.

Another client, Henry (the film director) seemed to take issue with the 'for your professional advantage' reason for networking:

Client: It seems so fake just to approach someone to be friendly in an insincere way, just for an ulterior motive.

Coach: What specifically is fake about it?

Client: Just to go after the one person in the room you know is the most use to you is fake.

Coach: How do you know they are the 'one person'?

It's interesting how we sometimes focus on what we perceive to be the 'bull's-eye' forgetting the rest of the target.

The idea behind networking is that you are never more than six degrees of separation (steps) from anyone in the world (or Kevin Bacon if you're an actor!)

So for example, if you know eight people, who know eight more people each, who in turn know eight more people. Then you are only two steps from having connections with 584 people! How useful would that be in your career?

When faced with a room of people how do you know who or what someone else knows?

Once Henry realised this, he could stop concentrating on the one most useful contact. He was able to relax, mingle and meet lots of new people.

As the father of positive psychology, Mihaly Csikszentmihalyi said:

> *"Of all the virtues we can learn, no trait is more useful, more essential for survival, and more likely to improve the quality of life than the ability to transform adversity into an enjoyable challenge."*

For Craig, it was the prospect of meeting an important director that was the daunting task. We worked to change the task to make it fun and to meet as many new people as possible. As a result he met lots of new interesting people including the director who became a key connection for him.

CHAPTER 26

Managing criticism

For all of us and particularly for those in creative roles, dealing with criticism can be an issue. Some even find dealing with praise an equally troubling process.

Perhaps it's not even the external judgments that concern you. Eloise Ristad in her book 'A Soprano on Her Head' talks about facing your internal judges, and the mix of people from your past who join forces inside you and tell you how bad you are!

One powerful way to sort out your internal judges is to laugh at them; pretend they have a silly voice (perhaps your favourite cartoon character) or a silly hat. Or better still, both. You can reason with them as their intention is ultimately for your own good; they are just going about it the wrong way. Ask your internal judges:

What is your purpose for criticising me?

What would be the consequence if you praised and encouraged me?

However, laughing or negotiating with external judges is unlikely to be an option. I worked on a different approach with one of my clients.

Maria was a budding author who wanted to understand the conflicting praise and criticism she was receiving. The information she had from different sources seemed completely contradictory:

Coach: How do you know which to believe?

Client: I would like to believe the praise, but the criticism brings me down.

Coach: How useful is this criticism and praise?

Client: It isn't because it is confusing!

I wondered what is the value of criticism, or for that matter praise, if it is not accurate or useful:

Coach: How can you judge which information is useful?

Client: When I think about who is giving me the criticism. I am not sure how qualified they are to pass judgment; I don't think they have ever had any work published.

Coach: What else?

Client: I could ask what is their motivation for criticising or praising me?

Think about praise and criticism simply in terms of feedback and more specifically 'useful feedback'. Realise that both positive and negative feedback can be useful if it's from a 'useful source'.

From a useful source, praise tells you what you are doing well; and criticism highlights areas where you could be better.

Of course there is useless feedback. Sadly a lot of feedback is useless! So when you find a source (for example, a teacher, mentor, coach, agent, manager, friend, etc.) who provides useful feedback, nurture them and hold on to them. They are worth their weight in gold.

And remember the words of polymath Benjamin Franklin:

> *"Any fool can criticise, condemn, and complain. And most fools do."*

CHAPTER 27

Finding a mentor

Finding a mentor can be very useful but some people are unsure of the value of one and often don't understand the difference between a mentor and a coach.

A mentor is a senior person in a particular field that guides a more junior person, based on their experience. Whereas a performance coach is an expert in high performance coaching, who works with clients to ensure they are performing at their best in all aspects of their life, and helps them achieve their dreams and desires. When a client asks me to be their mentor, I help them find the ideal people to assist them.

I was coaching Nicola, a TV editor who wanted to move into feature films, which she perceived as a big leap in her career development. In one of our sessions, she decided she would write to senior film editors she admired and ask them for a short meeting to get some help.

Afterwards we explored the advice she had been given, which she realised was based on experience from starting in the industry many years ago. For example, the media and entertainment industry, like many, has undergone significant technological changes and therefore some of the advice Nicola received was no longer relevant.

Analysing this further, she realised that her goal to move into film drama was not such a big leap after all. Some of these senior film editors had even asked for her advice on how to get more TV work!

A useful consequence for Nicola was that having met a number of very experienced film editors and developed a good relationship with them, she broadened her network

significantly. Within a few months she had started editing her first feature film.

Who are the senior and experienced people you admire?

What will you learn from them if you meet them for a coffee?

Once you have a mentor's perspective and advice, you can start to look at it from your point of view, whilst understanding that your journey will be unique to you.

There is an interesting quote from an unknown author,

> *"We tend to see our own experiences as the normal process, so we are often amazed that anyone could have taken a different path. But when we do meet up, it's always fascinating to compare notes about the different ways to get there."*

CHAPTER 28

Taking the next step

I have noticed that there is a common misunderstanding that coaching is only for people who have problems.

Most believe they understand the role of a coach in sport, but you may not be aware that the coaches to the most successful sports people are primarily coaching the player's mental attitude, rather than their techniques.

Many are surprised to hear that most senior executives have a coach. Executive coaches focus on the mental attitude and performance of each client.

At the first meeting with Olivia (the actress), I learned that she had been seeing a voice coach, a method-acting coach and a movement coach, who were all working with her to improve her techniques. But she still wasn't getting the right offers of work!

As a performance coach, I worked with Olivia to explore what was preventing her from winning the work she wanted. We built a plan to improve her networking and marketing skills, change her agent, modify her approach and attitude to auditions, and most importantly create a vision of her dreams and desires of her future in both the short and long term.

You may be wondering right now:

I have read the book, answered the questions, done the visualisations and exercises, what do I need to do now to achieve my dreams and desires?

Remember the chapters that talked about improving your self awareness, writing your goals down, discovering what you are passionate about, removing your limiting beliefs, achieving self-motivation and not giving up. Think how you have learned the power of planning, listening, networking and positive thinking.

There are many very talented people looking to achieve success and the competition is very intense (particularly in the media and entertainment industry). In my experience the difference between those who achieve their dreams and desires and those who do not, is their mental attitude.

As we have discovered, your mental attitude shows up in your internal dialogue, visualisations and emotions; and has a direct impact on the language you use and your behaviour.

The next step is for you to take action to make changes to your old habits, and transform them into new ones that will enhance your performance.

Maybe the next step for you will be to find a performance coach who will listen to what you say and observe all you do, provide feedback and ask the specific questions so that you can change the way you think, talk and perform, thus enabling you to 'RELEASE THE STAR WITHIN YOU'.

Printed in the United Kingdom
by Lightning Source UK Ltd.
115504UKS00001B/55-93